JAPAN
SUPERPOWER OF THE PACIFIC

DISCOVERING our HERITAGE

by Tony Zurlo

dP | **DILLON PRESS**
New York

Maxwell Macmillan Canada
Toronto

Maxwell Macmillan International
New York Oxford Singapore Sydney

Acknowledgments

I wish to thank the following people for their help, information, and encouragement while writing this book: Sue Pittman and Joy Johnson of the St. Marys, Ohio, library; Seiichi Suzuki, Nobue Jansen, Anne Carrell of the Japan National Tourist Organization, Dallas, and Hiroko Falty.

Photographs are reproduced through the courtesy of : The Japanese National Tourist Organization, Senator Daniel K. Inouye's congressional office, Tiffany Nicely, the National Japanese American Historical Society, and Tony Zurlo.

Library of Congress Cataloging-in-Publication Data

Zurlo, Tony.
    Japan, superpower of the Pacific / by Tony Zurlo.
        p. cm. — (Discovering our heritage)
    Includes bibliographical references and index.
    Summary: Examines the geography, history, culture, and people of Japan.
    ISBN 0-87518-480-4
    1. Japan—Juvenile literatre. [1. Japan.] I. Title. II. Series.
DS806.Z87 1991
952—dc20   91-15412

Dillon Press
Macmillan Publishing Company
866 Third Avenue
New York, NY 10022

Maxwell Macmillan Canada, Inc.
1200 Eglinton Avenue East
Suite 200
Don Mills, Ontario M3C 3N1

Macmillan Publishing Company is part of the Maxwell Communication Group of Companies.

First edition
Printed in the United States of America
10   9   8   7   6   5   4   3   2   1

JAPAN

Contents

Fast Facts about Japan

Official Name: Japan. Also *Nippon* or *Nihon* ("Source of the Sun")

Capital: Tokyo

Location: An island country off the northeastern coast of the Asian continent; to the northwest across the Sea of Japan is South Korea; China lies to the west

Area: 146,690 square miles (381,394 square kilometers); the four major islands are Honshu, Hokkaido, Shikoku, and Kyushu. Today, the Ryukyu Islands (Okinawa) are also a part of Japan; *Greatest distances:* northeast-southwest—1,500 miles (2,400 kilometers); at its widest point, the major island, Honshu, is 190 miles (307 kilometers) wide

Elevation: *Highest*—Mount Fuji, 12,388 feet (3,776 meters above sea level); *Lowest*—sea level, along the coast

Population: 123 million (1989 estimate); *Distribution*—76 percent urban; 24 percent rural. *Density*—826 persons per square mile (317 persons per square kilometer)

Form of Government: Constitutional monarchy; *Head of State*—His Imperial Majesty, the Emperor; *Head of Government*—Prime Minister

Important Products: *Agriculture*—rice, soybeans, tea; *Industry*—cameras, automobiles, electric and electronic devices, ships, textiles, steel

Basic Unit of Money: Yen

Major Languages: Japanese, English

Major Religions: Shinto, Buddhism

Flag: Red circle against a white background; the red circle represents the sun

National Anthem: *Kimigayo* ("The Reign of Our Emperor")

Major Holidays: New Year's Day—January 1; Children's Festival—May 5; Emperor's Birthday—December 23

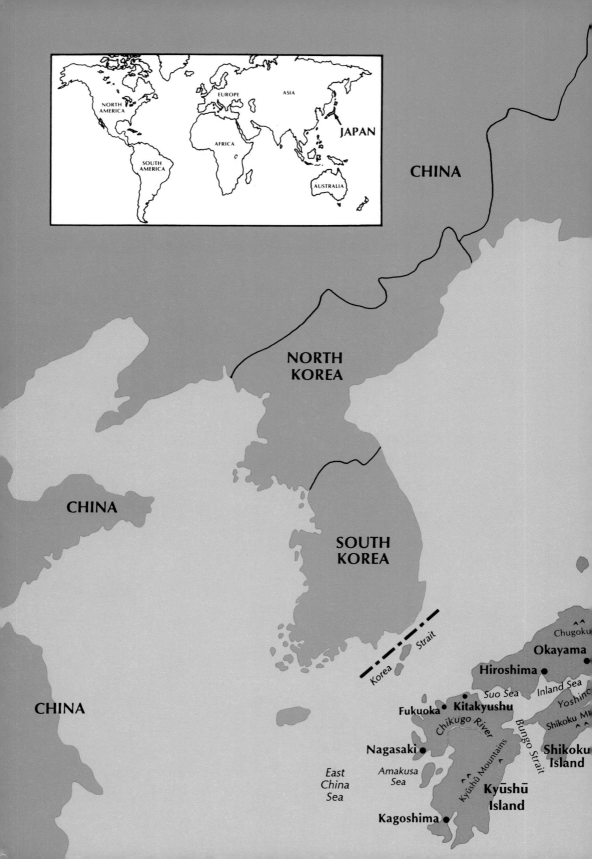

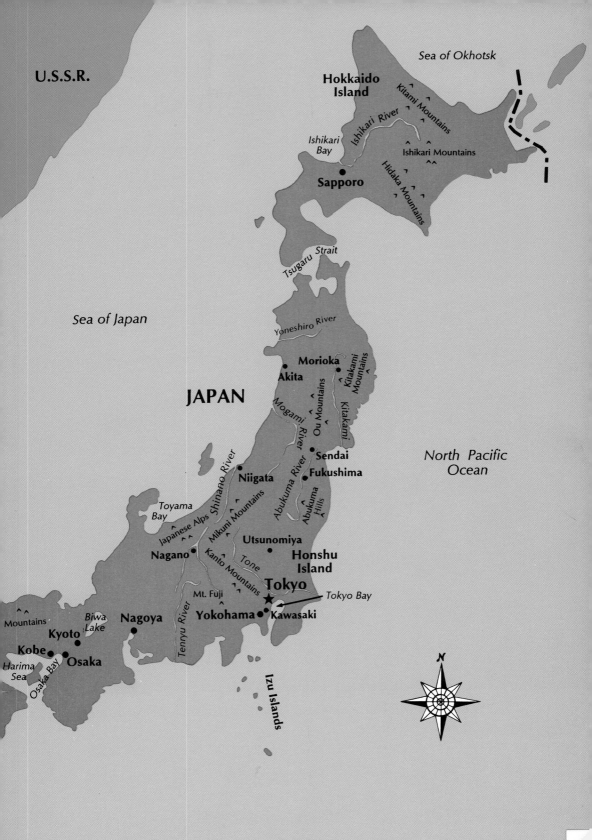

Fast-food restaurants, such as McDonald's, are a common sight in Japan.

1. Mountains and McDonald's

From six o'clock in the morning until nearly midnight, cars stream along the streets of Tokyo. People crowd the sidewalks, hurrying between shops, restaurants, businesses, and apartments. Above the crowds, neon signs flash on and off, advertising countless products, from expensive cameras to designer jeans.

In the middle of all this hustle and bustle is a peaceful four-hundred-year-old castle—the Imperial Palace, home of Japan's emperor. Many carefully groomed gardens, cherry trees, and walkways surround the castle. Beyond the gardens sparkles the modern backdrop of neon lights and McDonald's restaurants. This is Japan—a country rich in its cultural blend of East and West.

Islands in the Pacific

Tokyo, the capital, lies on the eastern shore of Honshu, the largest island in Japan. The country is made up of four major islands—Honshu, Hokkaido, Shikoku, and Kyushu—and thousands of smaller islands. The nation lies in the North Pacific Ocean—east of China and Korea. From north to south, the four major islands measure 1,744 miles (2,790 kilometers) in length, and the country's

Streets are always busy in Tokyo—a city of more than 8 million people—no matter what time of day or night.

widest point, in Hokkaido, is only 280 miles (about 450 kilometers) wide.

Almost half of Japan's 123 million people live near or along the Pacific coastline of Honshu. This area, about 343 miles (553 kilometers) long, is often compared to the area between Boston and Washington, D.C. Both have very high populations, are crisscrossed by hundreds of highways and railroads, and are centers of business and industry.

Tokyo, with its more than 8 million people, is the nation's largest city. Historians agree that as long ago as

1715, more than a million people lived in Tokyo, making it the largest city in the world at that time. Today, Tokyo is one of three large cities along Tokyo Bay. Yokohama—18 miles (28.8 kilometers) south of Tokyo—is the major seaport for Japan. Between these two cities is Kawasaki. More than 12 million people live in these three cities.

An equal number of people live in the area of central Honshu near the Inland Sea. Three cities—Osaka, Kobe, and Kyoto—are crowded together in a radius of about 50 miles (80 kilometers) and each of them has a population of about 2 million people. Nagoya, another city of 2 million, lies between Osaka and Tokyo.

North of Honshu lies Hokkaido, Japan's second largest island. Hokkaido has long, cold winters. With heavy snowfall throughout the island for almost six months each year, this northern island is popular for its winter sports. Its capital, Sapporo, hosted the 1964 Winter Olympics.

South of Honshu is Shikoku, the smallest of the major islands. Shikoku is mainly a fishing and farming area. The island is famous for its terraced fruit groves and whirlpools. Between Honshu and Shikoku is the Inland Sea, a favorite vacation spot for the Japanese. The Inland Sea is dotted with thousands of tiny islands covered with pine trees.

The southernmost island is Kyushu. It has a sub-tropical climate, with areas of lush vegetation. It also has

many hot springs and active volcanoes. Two of the island's cities—Kokuoka and Kitakyushu—each have populations of more than 1 million.

The entire country of Japan is about the size of the state of California. With 123 million people living on its crowded islands, the nation is one of the most densely populated countries in the world.

The Japanese Alps

Japan is so mountainous that people can live on only 15 percent of the land. The mountains and the hills take up so much land that most of the people live on the coastal plains. This has added to the problems of an overcrowded population, but the people wouldn't trade their beautiful mountains for more space! The mountains throughout the country are a major part of its world-famous spectacular scenery.

Called the Japanese Alps, the mountains were formed thousands of years ago from volcanic eruptions. About sixty active volcanoes still exist today. Mount Fuji, Japan's highest and most famous mountain, is inactive. It last erupted in 1707, depositing six inches of ashes on Tokyo—75 miles (120 kilometers) away from the eruption.

The mountains affect the climate everywhere in Japan. In the summertime, they trap much of the moist air

An aerial view of the Inland Sea.

Japan is a beautiful, mountainous land.

and rainfall along the eastern coast, so the western side of the islands tends to be drier. In the winter, however, the mountains trap snow and bitterly cold temperatures along the western side, while the east has more pleasant conditions.

Japan's weather is similar to that of the eastern United States. The heaviest snows fall in Hokkaido and northwestern Honshu, often piling up to the rooftops of houses. Less snow falls in the eastern and southern areas of Japan. Tokyo gets less than ten inches of snow each year.

Much of Japan's climate is determined by warm ocean currents from the Pacific. The air, carrying moisture from the ocean, rises rapidly when it meets the mountains. Thus eastern Japan receives rain every month, especially in the summer.

In the winter, cold winds from Siberia in northern Asia cross the Sea of Japan and bring the cold temperatures and heavy snow to northwestern Japan. But the mountains block most of the extreme cold and snow from moving into eastern Japan.

Natural Disasters

Some of the rainfall comes from storms, called typhoons or hurricanes. Typhoons blow in from the Pacific Ocean in August and continue through September. They often strike Kyushu, and sometimes Honshu, too. Heavy rains, high tides, and fierce winds—winds as high as 150 miles per hour (240 kilometers per hour)—damage buildings and at times take human lives. One typhoon struck Ise Bay near Nagoya in central Honshu on September 26, 1959, killing 4,700 people and injuring 39,000 more.

Because Japan is located on the edge of a five-mile-deep ocean crack, it experiences another type of dangerous natural disaster—earthquakes. About 1,500 earthquakes are recorded each year, though most of them are harmless. The worst one in modern history occurred in Tokyo at noon on September 1, 1923. Thousands of buildings were destroyed and 130,000 people died.

Country Life, City Life

About one-fourth of Japan's people live in rural areas. Most of the people who live in the country are farmers, though some members of farm families work at nearby factories or commute to jobs in cities.

Japanese farmers use combines and other modern equipment to work their fields. Rice is still the country's most important crop, as it has been for centuries. Prices of rice and other agricultural products are protected by the government, so most farmers make a comfortable living. But now that more efficient farming methods are used—including expensive equipment and fertilizers— fewer people can afford to farm. Only 15 percent of Japan's population farms full-time today, a decrease from more than 50 percent in the 1940s.

The other three-fourths of Japan's population lives year-round in the nation's urban areas. Cities are so crowded that land prices have become the highest in the world, and it is very difficult for people to buy houses. Even in Tokyo, where the average household income is

Rice paddies.

more than $40,000 a year, people find it difficult to afford their own homes. Most Japanese live in much smaller houses and apartments than Americans. In the large cities, a single person with a good job often lives in a one-room apartment.

The cities are so crowded with buildings that empty land for development is hard to find. One way the Japanese solve this problem is by filling in rivers and

parts of the ocean to create new land. Osaka, for example, is building an international airport on top of a landfill, and Kobe recently built new islands for industrial and port development.

Many city dwellers choose not to own cars because of the crowded streets, too few parking places, and the added expense of buying and maintaining a car. Less than 60 percent of Japanese families own cars. Instead, people take subways and buses to where they want to go. Parents and children alike often spend two to four hours each day commuting between home and work or home and school. Fortunately, Japanese cities have efficient and inexpensive public transportation.

People who need to travel between cities take the *Shinkansen*, or the "bullet train." Every major population center in Japan is linked by rail. Japanese call their high-speed electric trains "bullet trains" because they travel at speeds as high as 150 miles per hour (240 kilometers per hour).

In 1989, a 14-mile-long (22.4-kilometer-long) tunnel under the Tsugaru Straits was completed, linking the tip of northern Honshu with Hokkaido. It now takes less than eleven hours to make the 731-mile-long (1,170 -kilometer-long) trip between Tokyo and Sapporo.

Many country and most city residents work in factories and industries. In the years since World War II, Japan has become an industrial giant. The nation is the

Harvested rice dries on the river bank, then these boats transport the rice to market.

The bullet train speeds by majestic Mount Fuji.

world's leading producer of cars, computers, cameras, ships, televisions, and VCRs. Japan also leads the world in the fishing industry and in almost all electronics. Steel and textile industries too have boomed, during the country's economic success since World War II.

A Democratic Country

After World War II, the United States helped Japan set up a democratic government with a two-house congress called the Diet. It has a House of Representatives with

The Diet building in Tokyo.

512 members who serve four-year terms and a House of Councillors with 252 members who serve six-year terms.

The government is led by a prime minister. He is not elected directly by the people. Instead, he is the leader of the political party that has the most officials elected across the nation. There are many political parties, but the Liberal Democratic Party (LDP) has held a majority in the Diet since the 1950s. All of the prime ministers since then have been members of the LDP. The current prime minister is Toshiki Kaifu.

Japan also has an emperor. Emperor Akihito is the

125th emperor of the country. In various times throughout
the nation's history, emperors have held great political
power. But today the role is only ceremonial, with no
political power at all. Modern-day Japanese emperors,
however, are important symbols of the nation's character—representing politeness, loyalty, courage, intel-
ligence, and hard work. Japanese people have always
honored these traits, no less so in their hectic, highly
successful society today.

2. The Japanese People

In the sixth and seventh centuries, the ideas of Chinese Confucianism entered Japan. The main idea in Confucianism was that people should try to work out their difficulties without upsetting each other. This philosophy taught compassion, trustworthiness, loyalty to superiors and elders, and proper behavior. These values helped the Japanese people to live in harmony and to avoid serious fights.

The people adopted these values centuries ago and still hold firmly to them today. Most modern-day Japanese try to be polite, kind, and proper to one another, in both their behavior and in their language.

When greeting each other, the Japanese bow. To show respect, a younger person always bows deeper than an older person. This rule also applies to people in business, politics, education, and all other areas of life. The person who is lower in rank or position bows lower than the other person. Even in department stores, uniformed attendants bow low and open doors for customers.

The Japanese also try to be polite and considerate when speaking with one another. When denying a request, for example, they try to avoid using the word "no." This word makes people feel tense, they believe. Instead, they might say, "I'll think about it." This helps prevent the other person from feeling rejected or from getting embarrassed. The Japanese call this "saving face."

Group Loyalty

Being on friendly terms with people is very important to the Japanese people and they try hard to be accepted by others. When they introduce themselves to a new person, they bow, tell their names, and then mention the organization to which they belong—perhaps their school or place of work. Businesspeople exchange cards with this information.

The Japanese do this because they have a strong association with groups. They feel a great deal of loyalty to their families, friends, peers, businesses, and country.

Americans tend to think first about what is best for the individual. But Japanese people believe that what is best for the group is most important. Many older Japanese worry that young Japanese people are becoming less concerned about the welfare of the group and more concerned about their individual selves. But by American standards, even "selfish" Japanese young people today have deep respect for their families, friends, school, and country.

A Nation of Readers and Writers

The Japanese people also have great respect for the written word. Almost all adults can read and write. Nearly every adult reads a newspaper every day, and about half of them spend more than an hour a day reading magazines and books.

Japanese children, too, read almost every day. Much of their reading is required school homework. But they also like to read *manga*, or "comics." Comics are popular with boys especially, and many grow up wanting to become cartoonists. Stories about Japanese history and legends are favorites in these comics. Also popular are "lesson" comics—stories that teach the virtues of loyalty, friendship, personal effort, and bravery. One popular series, called *Shonen Sunday*, is about brave heroes who conquer dangers and evil.

It is natural that this nation of avid readers has produced a number of top-notch writers. Japanese newspapers and magazines are recognized the world over for their excellence, and Japanese literature has been ranked among the world's best. Many Japanese poets and writers have achieved worldwide recognition for their skills in their crafts. In 1968, the Japanese writer Yasunari Kawabata won a Nobel Prize for literature. Two of his better-known novels are *Snow Country* and *Thousand Cranes*.

Like Kawabata, Yukio Mishima's books have been translated into several languages. Other well-known writers today include Fumiko Enchi, Akiko Yosano, and Machi Tawara. Tawara, a former schoolteacher, recently published her first book of poems, *Salad Anniversary,* and it has become one of Japan's all-time best-sellers.

Most Japanese people also write poetry. A very popular type of poem is *haiku.* A haiku poem is short—only three lines—and must relate in some way to one of the four seasons. The most famous haiku poet in history was Matsuo Bashō, who lived in Japan during the 1600s.

Shintoism and Buddhism

Haiku is just one of many areas in Japanese culture that reflects the people's deep respect for nature. Since the third and fourth centuries A.D., the Japanese have practiced a nature-oriented religion called Shintoism, which means "the way of the gods." Early Shintoists worshipped many gods that were found in parts of nature, such as mountains, rivers, crops, trees, and the seasons. The Shintoists' main god was the sun goddess. The leader of the people—the emperor—was also considered a god.

Although they no longer believe in these gods, the Japanese still hold festivals that were once associated with them. By maintaining these traditions, the people today appear to be more religious than they really are.

The Japanese still hold festivals in honor of gods and goddesses, although most of the people no longer believe in them.

Only a small minority of modern-day Japanese believe strongly in just one single religion, such as Shintoism. Most participate in ceremonies from both Shintoism and Buddhism. For example, many Japanese want to be married by a Shinto priest, but prefer Buddhist funerals. However, in their personal lives, the majority of Japanese do not follow very closely the teachings of either religion.

Buddhism—a religion that stresses a life of virtue and wisdom—came to Japan from China and Korea in about A.D. 550. During the next thousand years, many

One of the many Buddhist temples in Japan.

different branches of Buddhism spread throughout Japan. Some, such as Shinshu or Pure Land (Jodo) and Zen, are still practiced today. Buddhist temples are popular places to visit on Japanese holidays, when the people offer prayers for their ancestors. But young Japanese people today visit temples mainly to show respect for tradition rather than to demonstrate their religious beliefs.

Flower Arranging

A popular art form in Japan also reflects the people's love of nature—flower arranging. Millions of Japanese practice *ikebana*, or "flower arranging." There are ikebana schools all across Japan. Most Japanese girls, and many boys, learn this art.

Skilled flower arrangers understand that they can only suggest what nature is like; they cannot create nature. Flowers are arranged in three basic positions—the highest flower represents heaven, the middle flower represents humans, and the lowest flower represents earth. More than 3,000 methods of arranging exist today, but all are ways of showing the relationships between heaven, humans, and earth.

Traditional and Popular Arts

Flower arranging is just one of many traditional Japanese arts that remains popular in the country today. *Noh* and *Kabuki* are centuries-old dramatic art forms that have remained popular. Noh began in the late fourteenth century as entertainment for court families, and Kabuki developed in the seventeenth century. Today, these plays are still performed in theaters throughout Japan.

In Noh drama, actors wear masks and chant their lines, presenting stories from Japanese history and mythology. Usually the topics are about the vanity of life or the involvement of gods in the daily lives of the upper class. Kabuki stories are about the everyday lives of merchants and other city people. Kabuki actors wear colorful costumes and makeup, and perform in exaggerated and lively movements. Today, many Japanese movies and television shows are made from Kabuki stories.

The Japanese make many movies other than those with Kabuki plots. The Japanese movie industry is one of the most prosperous in the world. It is famous for science fiction and adventure movies. Akira Kurosawa has directed some of the most successful Japanese adventure movies, and his *The Seven Samurai* was the model for the American film *The Magnificent Seven*. In 1990, Kurosawa received an Academy Award for his international reputation as a director. Another form of popular movie in Japan is the disaster film, with special effects showing earthquakes and monsters. The series of movies featuring the monster lizard Godzilla are Japanese-made.

The Japanese enjoy American films, too. In the 1980s, three of the most popular movies in Japan were American-made: *E.T., Jaws,* and *Star Wars.* Today, some American movie stars are so popular in Japan that they are asked to do commercials for Japanese television. Eddie Murphy holds the record for being paid the largest sum of money to act in a Japanese commercial.

The Japanese are also fond of American and European music, especially jazz and classical works. But they also have a long tradition of their own folk and instrumental music. Two of the more popular traditional instruments are the *shakuhachi*, a seven-holed bamboo flute, and the *koto*, a stringed instrument. Japan has a number of professional koto orchestras, such as one directed by Yoshio Hiratsuka. His Korei Society Koto Band plays both traditional and modern Japanese music to audiences all over the world.

Most young people in Japan listen to the latest rock music. Rock concerts and music videos are very popular. Japanese young people sing along with rock stars from around the world, such as Madonna, Michael Jackson, Phil Collins, Sting, and U2. Seiko Matsuda is Japan's own "princess of pop." In 1990, Seiko had fourteen number one albums and twenty-five straight number one songs on the Japanese pop charts.

Besides going to movies and listening to rock music, young Japanese watch a great deal of television—between three to five hours a day. They watch so much television that they are known as the *terebikko*, or "TV kids." One show they watch is the weekly cartoon "Sazasesan," which features problems faced in the homes of Japanese families today. Japanese people of all ages also enjoy watching game shows, sports events, and comedies.

Sometimes the Japanese are critical of themselves for allowing so much American culture to influence their own. But they also know that if new ideas will make their lives more comfortable and happy, they are open to change.

3. Emperors, Samurais, and Shoguns

Very little is known about the people who lived on the Japanese islands before the third century A.D. But scientists believe the earliest people lived by fishing and hunting on Honshu between 8000 and 300 B.C.

Beginning around A.D. 200, many invaders came from Korea, bringing Chinese and Korean culture with them. Through the next few centuries, they mixed with the original Japanese people and established a powerful clan in the Yamato Plain near Nara.

All Japanese emperors since then have claimed to be direct descendants of the Yamato clan. Historians agree that the first emperor reigned sometime between A.D. 200 and 400.

Prince Shotoku and His Reforms: A.D. 574–794

Throughout Japan's history, emperors were rarely involved with political decisions. They were considered directly related to the gods and therefore too holy to worry about everyday matters such as government. Their realm was more in the spiritual world.

Instead, powerful families ran the government. One of Japan's greatest leaders was Prince Shotoku Taishi, who lived between 574 and 622. Shotoku came from the clan in Nara. As regent, or advisor, to the emperor or empress, he controlled the government. He was also the first official to write down laws for the country.

Shotoku sent ambassadors to China to study its culture. China was undergoing a great cultural revival in the arts and in trade with Europe. Shotoku's representatives returned to Japan with reports of China's great architecture and elaborate cities. The reports impressed Shotoku and he decided to adopt the Chinese system of government, which had strong imperial rule. He believed that increasing the power of the emperor would help Japan become as prosperous as China.

Shotoku introduced new policies that made court officials follow the emperor's wishes more closely. These policies, called the Taika Reform laws, built a strong government which controlled every part of life in Japan. The laws included setting up relief for the poor; helping maintain bridges, roads, and Shinto shrines; establishing uniform weighing and measuring of products; and controlling the arts and industries.

Fujiwara Rule

Before 794, every time a new government came into power, the capital city was moved to the town of the new leader. In an attempt to give the government a permanent home, the Japanese built a new capital at Heian, now known as Kyoto. In 794, the emperor's home was moved from nearby Nara to Heian.

Powerful aristocratic families continued to rule the country. In the 800s, the Fujiwara family emerged as the strongest clan and it ruled Japan for about 300 years. During Fujiwara rule, emperors lost all real political power, though they still officially reigned.

The family's most important member was Fujiwara-no-Michinaga, who lived between 966 and 1027. He gained even more influence by arranging marriages between his daughters and emperors. His grandson by his first daughter's marriage to Emperor Ichijō became Emperor Goichijo. Then Fujiwara-no-Michinaga arranged for his third daughter to marry his grandson, Emperor Goichijo. With his family on the throne, he was able to rule as regent for more than twenty years.

Civil Wars: 1192–1600

Between the twelfth and seventeenth centuries, civil wars kept Japan divided. While emperors continued as the religious and symbolic heads of the nation, aristocratic clans fought for control of the land. The Minamoto family won the first series of wars in 1192. They moved their government to Kamakura, but the emperor remained in Kyoto.

In 1336, the Minamotos lost their power to another family, the Ashikaga. This family moved the government back to Kyoto. A civil war continued for two more centuries.

During these five centuries of unrest, Japan was ruled by a military government. Military leaders or generals called *shoguns* controlled the country. A shogun was the head of the family in power. Although emperors still reigned, they appointed each new shogun and the shoguns were the true rulers of Japan.

The shoguns divided the countryside into regions, and each region was governed by a *daimyo*, or lord. Daimyos always swore allegiance to the shogun.

Daimyos hired *samurai*, or warriors, to protect their regions, estates, crops, and the peasants who worked for them. The samurai received incomes from their daimyo in rice or land or, in later years, money.

Samurai lived by a "code of the warrior" called *Bushido*. Over time, this code became the model for Japanese values. By this code, the samurai lived simple lives dedicated completely to protecting their daimyo. They were expected to be very strong both mentally and physically to overcome their enemies in battle. To prepare themselves for this, they experienced extreme tests to learn how to withstand pain. The courage and bravery of the samurai warriors soon made them the most respected class in society.

These men today remember their ancestors by wearing traditional samurai warrior garments.

Japan Unifies: 1500–1600

Three shoguns led Japan back to national unity: Oda Nobunaga, Toyotomi Hideyoshi, and Tokugawa Ieyasu. Before Nobunaga died in a military campaign in 1582, he had unified the eastern half of Japan. He also opened Japan to European ideas by allowing Christians to start missions and by encouraging Japanese trade with Portugal and Holland.

When Nobunaga died, Hideyoshi became the new military leader. Because he wasn't a handsome man, people nicknamed him "Monkey." He was, however, such an excellent military man that he was promoted rapidly from foot soldier to general. Hideyoshi defeated an army led by one of Nobunaga's old enemies and took control of the entire country. As shogun, he surveyed and reassigned land, so the government could keep an accurate account of taxes. He also seized all peasants' weapons to prevent them from revolting.

Tokugawa Rule: 1600–1868

As an ally of Hideyoshi, Tokugawa Ieyasu had been given control of Edo, known as Tokyo today. After Hideyoshi's death, Ieyasu set out to complete the unification of the entire country. But another of Hideyoshi's former generals, Ishida Mitsunari, wanted to take control of Japanese lands. In 1600, Ieyasu's army of 80,000 defeated Mitsunari's 100,000 troops at the battle of Sekigahara, just north of Nagoya. Ieyasu was now the new shogun.

Ieyasu and other Japanese leaders soon became distrustful of Europeans and their religion, Christianity. With the growing popularity of Christianity in Japan, Japanese leaders began to suspect Christians of having political intentions. Ieyasu and his followers began to persecute and kill thousands of Japanese Christian converts.

The imperial palace in Tokyo was mainly built and expanded in the early 1600s, during Tokugawa Ieyasu's rule.

Fear of foreign influence became so great that leaders passed laws making it a crime for a Japanese person to leave the country or for a foreigner to enter Japan. The only outside contact allowed was on a tiny human-made island called Dishima, in Nagasaki harbor. About a dozen Dutch merchants were allowed to keep supplies there.

In the early years of Tokugawa rule, daimyos began to build large castles to show off their wealth and prestige. Craftsmen and merchants moved near these castles where they knew they could get jobs from the daimyos. Soon, villages grew up around some of the larger castles.

Samurai warriors kept order on the grounds of the estates and their surrounding croplands.

To ensure loyalty to the shoguns, daimyos had to live alternate years at the shogun's palace in Edo. Their families had to stay there permanently. As a result, daimyos supported two residences. Trips back and forth took up most of their time and were expensive. Daimyos were too busy to plot rebellion against the shogun.

Under the Tokugawa clan's reign, Japan had two and a half centuries of peace. The life of common people improved. Major highways and hotels were built to link the new towns. Education, which was popular with the samurai, spread to the general population.

Ieyasu and other Tokugawa shoguns tried to rule Japan without allowing any outside influences. But the world was changing. By the 1800s, Japan had reached a critical point in its history. Its leaders began to realize that European and American powers were expanding across the world.

These two great industrial nations were exploring and taking over colonies in Africa and Asia. Soon, the shoguns knew, Europe and America would be making demands on Japan. The Japanese really had only two choices: to allow foreign ideas to enter Japan, then begin to modernize so that the country could become strong enough to defend itself or to risk the Europeans or Americans taking control of Japan.

This castle in Japan was built by a daimyo in the 1600s.

During the peaceful Tokugawa rule, progress boosted the economy and the life of the common people improved.

The Opening of Japan: 1853–1868

Japan's contact with other nations began in the 1850s. American naval commodore Matthew C. Perry sailed four ships into Edo (Tokyo) Harbor in July of 1853. Two ships were steam powered, and they blew bellows of black smoke into the air. The Japanese called the squadron "Black Ships" and the sailors "hairy barbarians."

Perry's instructions were to make a trade treaty with Japan. However, the Japanese who met him at the ship refused Perry's first request to meet with high Japanese officials. It was still the law to bar all foreigners from Japan.

The United States decided that Perry should return with a strong show of military force. The following February he arrived outside Tokyo with nine heavily armed ships and 1,600 men. This strong military show impressed the Japanese.

To convince the Japanese further of superior American technology, Perry brought some unique presents. One was a telegraph wire. He stretched out a half mile of wire and sent a message through it. Some Japanese people raced to the other end to wait for the message. When they reached the end of the wire, they were astonished to find that the message had already arrived.

Another present was a train, complete with 350 feet (nearly 106.7 meters) of circular track. It was smaller than a full-size train but large enough for adults to ride in. The Japanese took turns riding along at 20 miles (32 kilometers) per hour, their robes flying in the wind.

Now the Japanese were convinced that Americans had superior technology and were capable of destroying Japan. At last, Perry met with Japanese officials and they signed a treaty that allowed the United States to send a consul, or representative, to live in Japan. Soon the American consul, Townsend Harris, negotiated a full treaty that opened up ports to American trade.

Meiji Restoration: 1868–1912

Before the opening to Western trade, however, a great debate raged in Japan. The tendency among the great daimyos, who advised the shoguns, was to keep out the West. Influential daimyos in southern Japan challenged European fleets in battles. The result was disastrous for Japan. The Europeans destroyed complete Japanese forts and cities in the battles.

Realizing the extreme power of the West, the leaders from these southern Japanese lands decided that Japan had to make compromises with the West. Only then, they realized, could Japan learn the technology necessary to build a modern nation. Otherwise, Japan could lose its independence to European control.

In 1868, a sixteen-year-old prince was declared emperor. He took the name Meiji, meaning "Enlightened Rule," and became the symbol for turning Japan into a modern world power. As usual, politicians ran the government, but the new emperor attended all of the meetings and was more active in guiding the government than any emperor in more than eight hundred years.

After the legislature was reorganized, it immediately eliminated the positions of shogun, daimyo, and samurai. The daimyo and samurai received pensions, and many of the samurai became businessmen or politicians.

Japanese officials traveled to Europe and the United

States to study Western forms of education, government, industry, law, and the military. The Japanese army and navy ministries were modeled on Germany's, and the court and legal system were adapted from both Germany and France. American business leaders were brought to Japan to help set up a modern industrial base. Fewer than thirty-five years after Meiji became emperor, Japan had built a modern power strong enough to compete with other advanced countries in the world.

The Rise of Militarism: 1900–1945

As Japan became equal to the West industrially, the military wanted to show its new strength. Only fifty years earlier, it had been completely embarrassed by its weakness against Western powers. Now the Japanese military wanted to prove that Japan was a major world power. To do this, the military decided to copy the West by taking control of colonies. The areas it sought were in China, Southeast Asia, and the Pacific islands. The military called its plan the Greater East Asia Co-prosperity Sphere.

As early as 1904, Japan's military had convinced the government to move into northeast Asia. Japan declared war on Russia, which occupied portions of Manchuria. Japan won, becoming the first modern Asian nation to defeat a major European power.

Expansion continued. In 1910, Japan took over Korea. During World War I, Japan sided with the United States, France, and Great Britain against Germany. When Germany lost, Japan received even more territory, including parts of China that were formerly ruled by Germany.

In the 1930s, a worldwide depression seriously damaged the Japanese economy. Conditions were so bleak that some people ate tree bark to stay alive. A few people who couldn't feed their children sold them to families who could afford to raise them. Now the military completely took over the government, because the civilian government was too weakened by the crippled economy to rule.

The military claimed that by taking over areas outside the country, Japan would have more space to develop economically. In 1932, Japan took over the rest of Manchuria. It increased steel and iron production in the plants already operating there. Then, in 1937, Japan moved into northern China. The Chinese were fighting their own civil war, so Japan easily took control of their lands.

Five years later, on December 7, 1941, Japan bombed Pearl Harbor near Honolulu, Hawaii. This brought the United States into World War II. World War II was a costly war for Japan. The nation lost more than 75 percent of its ships and all of its ports were destroyed. Ninety

Hiroshima Peace Memorial Park today. The destroyed dome building in the background was directly under the bomb blast.

major cities were severely damaged by American fire-bombs. On August 6, 1945, the United States dropped an atomic bomb on Hiroshima, Japan, killing or injuring nearly 130,000 people. Three days later, another atomic bomb was dropped on Nagasaki. By the end of World War II, half of the industry in Japan had been destroyed.

Postwar Prosperity

When World War II ended in 1945, Emperor Hirohito urged the Japanese people to work hard to rebuild their war-torn nation. The people listened and applied their energies to rebuilding their country. By the 1960s, Japan was once again competing economically with the wealthy countries of the West.

Part of modern Japan's complex formula for success lies in its constitution, which says that the country will never again start a war. Modern Japan has only a small military for self-defense. Most of the nation's budget is spent on building up businesses instead of buying military equipment.

Another part of the formula for success comes from the close cooperation between government and business. The government's Ministry of International Trade and Industry (MITI) sets goals for businesses. It also gathers information on economic trends and informs business leaders so they can make better business decisions.

Certain businesses set examples for the rest of industry. Six large companies own about 16 percent of the total business market. Their origins go back at least to the 1800s, and some can be traced to the start of the Tokugawa period. The groups are Mitsubishi, Mitsui, Sumitomo, Fuyo, Sanwa, and Dai-ichi Kangin.

Typical large businesses rarely operate in one field. For example, Mitsubishi is involved in making products as varied as automobiles, textiles, and electrical machinery; it also has large investments in banking, imports, and real estate. Usually, a company that is mainly involved in one industry will have its own branch companies that supply parts and services to the main company. An automobile maker such as Honda has branch businesses that provide seat covers, tires, windshield wipers, radios, brakes, and other supplies for automobiles.

Japanese management techniques also help explain the nation's economic success. The Japanese custom of group loyalty is important. A business worker is guaranteed lifetime employment, company recreational facilities, dormitories to live in, banks for checking accounts and loans, and other services.

The Japanese work long hours and maintain strict loyalty toward their employers. By making their companies successful, they have helped create one of the world's leading industrial nations. By combining a sense of group loyalty with an openness to outside ideas, the Japanese people have built their country into a great power twice in the past 125 years!

4. Tales Told in Japan

The early Japanese people believed that supernatural beings or gods controlled different parts of nature—such as the sun's heat and the falling rain. Through the centuries, many legends and tales were invented about these gods. The most important supernatural being was Amaterasu, the goddess of the sun, who sent light and warmth to the earth. She lived in heaven with the other gods. A famous Japanese legend suggests that she was the great-grandmother of Japan's first emperor—Jimmu-tenno.

Amaterasu, the Sun Goddess

According to this legend, Amaterasu had a mischievous brother named Susanowo, who was also a god. Susanowo loved to play tricks on the other gods and goddesses, especially on his sister Amaterasu.

One day, he played a very mean trick on his sister. He killed a horse and tossed the skin into Amaterasu's hall, where she and her maidens were weaving. The blood-splattered skin horrified and insulted the women.

Amaterasu usually tried to be patient with her brother's mischievous ways, but this time he had gone too far and she refused to forgive him. Disgusted with Susanowo, Amaterasu retreated into a cave. Because she was the source of the world's sunlight, the earth grew dark. Worried that the sun would never return, the other gods and goddesses dug up a tree and replanted it in the front of the cave. From its branches they hung a five-hundred-string necklace of amethyst and turquoise, and a large mirror.

The gods and goddesses began to laugh loudly and create a terrible ruckus outside the mouth of the cave. They knew this would make Amaterasu curious. Soon, she peeked outside, but the first things she saw were the sparkling necklace hanging from the tree and her bright image in the mirror. Charmed by the lovely necklace and her sunny mirror image, Amaterasu stepped outside the cave. Instantly, light returned to the world. The other gods and goddesses quickly roped off the cave's entrance so that Amaterasu could not go back inside and deprive the world of light anymore.

Meanwhile, the gods and goddesses had banished Susanowo from heaven for playing the cruel trick on his sister. In his exile, he wandered the countryside, until he came to Honshu, where he met an old couple. The man and woman sat by their cottage, weeping as if their hearts would break. Susanowo asked what made them cry so bitterly and they told him about a terrible eight-headed dragon that had eaten seven of their daughters. They had only one daughter left and the dragon was on its way to eat her, too!

Susanowo thought this story was sad indeed. "You have no need to cry," he assured the couple. "I am a god and I can help."

At once, Susanowo put his supernatural powers to work and turned the one remaining, beautiful daughter into a comb. Then he tucked the comb in his hair.

When the eight-headed dragon arrived at the cottage, each head began to drink greedily from one of the eight bowls of sake that Susanowo had left out for them. Susanowo's trick worked, and the dragon became very drunk and fell asleep. Susanowo killed the dragon while it slept, cutting off its heads and its tail.

Clunk! As Susanowo cut through the dragon's tail, his sword struck something hard. He quickly cut the tail open and found a beautiful silver sword inside, its handle studded with jewels.

Susanowo took the comb out of his hair and turned it back into the young woman. She and Susanowo were soon married and through the years they had many beautiful children.

Susanowo gave the jewel-studded silver sword to his sister to make up for the cruel trick he had played on her. But Amaterasu still could not forgive him. Instead of allowing her mischievous brother to rule over the earth any longer, she sent her grandson, Ninigi, to do so.

Amaterasu gave Ninigi three treasures to help in his rule—the silver sword, the amethyst necklace, and the large mirror.

Over time, these three treasures became the symbols of the Imperial family of Japan. Ninigi married the daughter of the sea god and they had many handsome children. One of their sons, Jimmu-tenno, became Japan's first emperor. Today, the sword, the necklace, and the mirror remain the symbols of the emperor and his family.

The One-Straw Millionaire

Through the centuries, the Japanese have been especially fond of Kannon, their goddess of mercy. Age-old legends and folktales are still told about this kind goddess who often granted wishes to the unfortunate.

"The One-Straw Millionaire" is a folktale that tells of a man who had such bad luck that he finally wanted to die. But he decided to pray one last time to Kannon for a little luck.

"You're my last hope," the man prayed. "I have no more food or money. And I can't get a job. Please send me just a little luck so I'll know that life is worth living."

After praying all day and night, the man was so tired he fainted. Kannon appeared to him in a dream. She told him that when he left the temple he would fall and that he should grab whatever was nearby. He should hold on to

This shrine in Tokyo honors Kannon, the goddess of mercy.

it, the goddess instructed, and walk toward the west.

When the man left the temple, he fell and grasped a piece of straw. While he was sitting on the ground wondering how a piece of straw could ever bring him luck, a horsefly landed on his shoulder. He caught the fly and tied it to the end of the straw.

The man decided to keep walking. Soon he met a woman carrying a crying baby boy. The baby stopped crying when he saw the fly, and the man gave the boy the straw and fly as a toy. The woman was poor, but she gave the man three tangerines to thank him.

Carrying the tangerines, he kept walking and met a young woman dying of thirst. He cut the tangerines and gave them to her. The nourishment saved her life, and as a reward, the woman gave him three rolls of fine silk. Could my luck be changing? the man wondered.

Next, he met a dangerous samurai standing over his dying horse. The samurai forced the man to exchange the silk for the horse. At first the man felt very unhappy, fearing his luck was again taking a turn for the worse. But he had sympathy for all living things, so he began to stroke the dying horse and pray for its recovery. Suddenly the horse jumped up and began nuzzling the man. He now owned a healthy horse!

A short distance away was a castle. The man walked over to the stables, and the attendants agreed to feed and water the horse. When the wealthy daimyo of the estate heard about the horse, he went immediately to bargain for it.

"Five hundred pieces of gold," he bargained. "A thousand pieces of gold!"

This was so much money that the poor man fainted.

"Bring some water for the man," the daimyo told his daughter.

The young woman recognized the man immediately. "This is the man who gave me the tangerines that saved my life!" she cried.

After praising the man's character, the daimyo offered

him his daughter's hand in marriage. The daimyo knew that his estate would be inherited by a worthy gentleman.

Kannon is indeed a merciful goddess, thought the man happily.

Hachisuke and the White Fox

Many Japanese stories are told about a fox that was a messenger for both gods and people. One popular folktale is about this fox and a daimyo, who lived on the western coast of Japan across the mountains from Kyoto.

One afternoon, this daimyo was out walking and he heard a terrible yapping. He saw a snow-white fox race around a corner, followed by four angry men. The men caught the fox and began to kick it.

"Stop! Don't hurt the poor animal," the daimyo demanded.

"But your lordship," they protested, "he kicked over everything in our store and ate our dried fish."

The daimyo paid the men for the damages and brought the fox home. When the fox became healthy again, the daimyo took it to the mountains and said, "Now listen, little one. Don't come back here stealing things from people. Understand? Go on home now." And from that day on the town was never again bothered by foxes.

One day the daimyo needed to send a message to the capital, Kyoto. The message had to be delivered within seven days or the daimyo and his family would be disgraced and ruined. But his messenger was sick, and no one else could make the journey in time.

Suddenly, a boy appeared at the castle door. "My name is Hachisuke," he said. "I heard your lordship needs a swift messenger. I am quite fast." The daimyo decided to send the boy, along with the letter tucked safely inside a box. The boy delivered the letter and returned with the reply in seven days.

To reward him, the daimyo appointed Hachisuke his chief messenger. On all of his journeys, Hachisuke had only one fear—being attacked by wild dogs.

One summer day, the daimyo realized that Hachisuke was almost three weeks late in returning from a trip. Worried, he gathered his servants, and they all saddled horses and set out to look for Hachisuke.

After days of searching in the mountains, they came across a white object lying in the forest. The daimyo jumped from his horse and ran over to it. He became pale and fell to his knees, saying, "Good heavens! The white fox." It had died lying over the letter box, as if trying to protect it. "Hachisuke!" cried the daimyo.

To repay the daimyo for saving its life, the fox had changed itself into a boy so he could help the daimyo. The fox lost its own life while serving its master.

Legends and stories such as "Hachisuke and the White Fox," "The One-Straw Millionaire," and

"Amaterasu, the Sun Goddess" help teach Japanese children today about their culture and heritage. Hearing these tales from their parents, grandparents, and teachers, young people learn about the traditions and beliefs of their ancestors.

5. Holidays, Festivals, and Celebrations

The Japanese celebrate national holidays or major festivals during every month of the year. Besides these, villages and cities frequently have their own festivals and celebrations.

Japanese holidays and festivals usually involve parades, parties, and merrymaking. Often, Shinto or Buddhist priests conduct services to honor the local patron gods. At many festivals, children participate in traditional games. Many people who come to watch the events dress up in traditional Japanese kimonos.

New Year's

Shogatsu, or "New Year's," is the main festival in Japan. The celebration begins during the Christmas season, a holiday that the Japanese have imported from the United States and Europe. Before Christmas, department stores are bright with decorations and lights, and sales appear everywhere. By Christmas Day, the school semester is over, and boys and girls crowd city sidewalks and stores to look at the displays.

Adults shop for presents which they call *oseibo* (year-end gifts), that they will give away at the end of

Many women and girls wear traditional kimonos during celebrations and festivals.

December. This is a way of thanking one another for favors during the year. Stores display year-end gifts to buy, such as food, soaps, and towels.

Large businesses hold *bonen-kai,* or "forgetting-the-year" parties. People are encouraged to forget worries and problems of the past year and to look with hope toward the new year.

Just before New Year's Day, people clean their houses thoroughly and try to pay off their debts. The front of many houses are decorated with *kadomatsu,* decorations of pine branches set in bamboo baskets and

The front of this home is decorated with kadomatsu *during the New Year's festival.*

tied with rice-straw rope. The pine represents health, strength, and a long life. The bamboo symbolizes strong character and rapid physical growth. A twisted straw rope is placed above the front door to bring good luck and keep evil out of the house.

On New Year's Eve, families watch popular television shows, visit shrines, and make last-minute preparations for the next day. At midnight, bells in Buddhist temples ring throughout the country. Every bell is rung 108 times, each ring standing for one of the 108 evil desires that a Buddhist must eliminate to live a pure life.

This torii *stands in water and visitors pass through the gate in a boat.*

Between New Year's Day and January 7, families visit shrines to pray for a good year. The ritual at a shrine is very simple. Visitors enter through a gate called a *torii*. A torii is usually painted red and is constructed of a crossbeam of wood—sometimes stone, concrete, or bronze—that is propped up by two vertical posts.

Beyond the torii, the visitors walk to a pool or basin to wash their hands and mouth. They approach the shrine, where they clap their hands twice to get the attention of the god. Then the visitors bow their heads and pray.

On New Year's Day, many adults wear traditional dress and visit people they received favors from during the year. Parents and relatives give children envelopes of money.

During the holiday, children fly kites, spin tops, and play *hagoita*, or "badminton." Another game they enjoy is called *Fukuwarai*. The outline of a girl's face is drawn on a piece of paper and the paper is placed in front of a blindfolded player. This player has to draw eyes, a nose, and a mouth on the paper face.

Another traditional New Year's activity is a card game called *Hyakunin isshu*. The Japanese have played this game for centuries. On each of fifty cards is a poem with a drawing of the poet. The concluding verses of these poems are on another set of fifty cards. These are spread out, faceup. A reader begins to read a poem, and the players try to find the card with the last verse of that poem. The player who picks the most "last-verse" cards is the winner.

Every New Year's, thousands of Japanese people participate in a national poetry-writing contest sponsored by the emperor. He selects a theme for writing *waka*—a type of poem with thirty-one syllables. In 1988, Emperor Hirohito selected "vehicle" as the theme. The judges received 28,015 entries, but only 13 were selected as winners. These were read over the radio, along with the emperor's poem, as every year he writes a poem, too.

Doll's Festival

Girls have their own special day on March 3, although it is not a national holiday. It is called *Hinamatsuri,* or the "Doll's Festival." A long time ago this festival was a purification rite—a way of getting rid of troubles. People would write their problems down and attach them to paper dolls, then float the dolls down the river. This is still practiced in several places in Japan today.

Parents give their girls sets of dolls on Hinamatsuri. The dolls are clothed in royal dress to represent the emperor and empress and their household. It is said that so much care is taken in making these dolls that every doll has its own soul. As many as twenty skilled carvers and painters work on each doll before it is sold in the stores.

On this day, girls ask their friends over for a party. They all sing songs and eat rice cakes prepared just for this occasion. The dolls are displayed on shelves in one part of a room. The top row is for the emperor and empress dolls. Below them—depending upon how many the family can afford—are a number of dolls dressed as women attendants, musicians, and dancers. On the bottom rows are tiny re-creations of fine furniture and musical instruments.

These girls dress in kimonos and play with their beautiful dolls during the Doll's Festival in March.

Children's Festival

May 5 is a national holiday called *Kodomo no hi*. Although the day is now set aside for both boys and girls, this festival was originally just for boys. Some Japanese, though, still call this holiday *Tango no Sekku*, or "Boy's Festival."

On this day, many families that have male children fly cloth banners outside their homes. The banners resemble carp swimming vigorously upstream. In Japan, the carp is considered a strong, courageous fish. The carp banners represent the sturdy, brave spirit that the Japanese believe boys must have to tackle difficulties in life.

Inside their houses, the families display samurai dolls dressed in armor. Miniatures of drums and other equipment used by the samurai in battle are also displayed. The samurai dolls suggest strength and fearlessness, traits the Japanese believe that boys must also have to be successful in life.

Cherry Blossom Viewing

One of the most popular celebrations in the spring is cherry blossom viewing. The five-petaled blossoms fill the parks and hillsides with color throughout the country. Sometimes it looks as if an artist has splashed entire hillsides with buckets of white and pink paint.

The annual flowering of the cherry tree gives the Japanese a feeling of spiritual renewal after the cold winter months. But the delicate blossoms' brief life spans also demonstrate how fast beauty and life seem to pass. The Japanese call this event *Hanami,* or "flower viewing."

Cherry trees begin to blossom in southern Japan in mid-March, but in northern Hokkaido they don't start until May 10 or later. Every day, television announcers give the dates and locations for the best blossom viewing. When the blossoms are in full bloom, the Japanese crowd parks to celebrate with picnics, singing, and dancing.

All Soul's

In most of Japan, All Soul's ceremonies are held in the middle of August. Between August 13 and 16, people welcome the souls of their dead ancestors back for a visit. The Japanese begin the festival by visiting the graves of their ancestors. Some people light "welcoming fires" in front of their houses. In most places dances are held. A stage is set up and people in traditional and modern dress dance through the streets and around the stage. After these celebrations, a large bonfire is burned to light the way for the ancestors' souls returning to the spirit world.

Several cities are famous for these celebrations, but the largest All Soul's festival is in Kyoto. Beginning at eight o'clock in the evening on August 16, a huge fire is lighted on the highest mountain peak near the city. At the same time, more than 10,000 paper lanterns with lighted candles are floated down the river to guide the souls back to their spirit world.

Shichigosan

Japan has many festivals for children, and usually the whole family participates. The most popular of these is *Shichigosan,* or "Seven-Five-Three Day." Every year on November 15, parents take their five-year-old sons and their three- and seven-year-old daughters to a Shinto shrine to pray for the health and happiness of the children. *Chitose-ame,* or "thousand-year candy," is sold at the shrine grounds. Eating this long red-and-white stick of candy is supposed to bring a thousand years of happiness to each child. Some families still dress in traditional kimonos for this celebration. Today, however, many dress in suits, skirts, and blouses for the ceremony.

Japanese holidays and festivals, such as Shichigosan, give the people a way to keep in touch with their traditional culture. Each month dozens of festivals are held throughout the country. Their popularity indicates that the Japanese are proud of their heritage and that they wish to preserve their customs for future generations.

6. The Japanese Family

Life for Japanese families has changed rapidly since the end of World War II. Families are smaller and homes have more modern conveniences. More women are working outside the home, too, and this has brought changes to many families.

Some of the old Japanese customs remain, however. Mothers are still mainly responsible for raising the children. Most fathers continue to work long hours each day, and often on Saturdays also, to make enough money to provide a comfortable home for their families.

Country Homes, City Homes

Whether Japanese families live in the city or the country, almost all are likely to have electricity and modern appliances. Most households have at least one television set, a refrigerator, an automatic washing machine, and a vacuum cleaner. About one-third have microwave ovens.

Older homes in rural areas are made from wood, although sometimes stone is used. Roofs are thatched or tiled, and the floor is usually dirt, covered only by mats. Today, however, wooden rural homes with thatched roofs are less common than they used to be. Many have

An aerial view of apartments in Kyoto.

been torn down and replaced with factories. Some industries are moving to the country to avoid expenses in the cities. These industries are also building houses and apartments with modern conveniences, where their rural factory workers can live.

Businesses located in both the country and the cities build dormitories for single and married workers. This inexpensive housing provides workers with room and board, as well as parks, gyms, swimming pools, golf courses, and tennis courts.

In the cities, where 75 percent of the population lives,

modern houses and apartments are commonplace. Yet they are expensive to buy or rent. A middle-income family is lucky to find a five- or six-room house or apartment. Because of the high demand for homes, a family might have to wait many years to find one that it can afford.

Tall apartment and business buildings dominate the urban Japanese landscape. But there are also many traditional Japanese homes in the cities. A traditional home is usually built away from the street. To enter the yard, people walk through a gate with a sliding door, down a path, and past a small garden. At the house, sliding doors open to a small entrance hall where the people take off their shoes and put on slippers. Wearing slippers helps keep the floors of the house clean.

The interior rooms of traditional homes are usually divided by lightweight screens made of wood and paper. By sliding these screens back and forth, the family can change the size of the rooms. Little children sometimes poke holes in the screens, and their parents have to replace the paper. In the summer, sliding doors are opened to allow breezes to circulate through the homes.

Heating traditional Japanese homes in the winter is difficult. *Hibachis*—metal or ceramic pots that contain burning charcoal—are sometimes used. But they only heat small areas.

Today, more than 90 percent of Japanese homes—

traditional and modern—have portable heaters and fans run by electricity or kerosene. These heaters are placed beneath a table in the main room, and the family gathers around to eat, read, and watch television. To help keep the heat in the central room, other rooms can be closed off with sliding doors.

At night, family members often sleep in the same room. They sleep on four-inch- (ten-centimeter) thick cotton mattresses called *futons* and cover themselves with quilts. In the morning, the futons are folded and placed in a storage area, so the room is not cluttered.

In large cities, where modern apartments and houses are common, many middle-class families are able to afford chairs, dining tables, and couches. A typical city apartment for a middle class family has five rooms—a bedroom, a living room that doubles as a second bedroom, a kitchen, a dining room, and a bath. Bathrooms are usually two rooms, one for the toilet and one for the bathtub or shower.

Raising Children

Japanese children are cuddled and waited on almost constantly. They grow up with a comfortable feeling of security but also with a feeling of dependency toward their parents. As a result, the Japanese have a lifelong desire to be emotionally protected and supported by

Walls in traditional Japanese homes are lightweight paper screens. This woman sits in front of a screen, preparing tea.

someone in authority. The word *amae* expresses this feeling. Students feel amae toward their teachers, employees feel it toward their executives, and athletes toward their coaches.

As they get older, children are pressured by their parents to behave well. They are taught never to embarrass their friends, and the worst offense they can commit is embarrassing their family. In disciplining their children, parents point out how their bad behavior can bring shame on the family and the children themselves. They often tell children who misbehave that they are not liked and that other people will laugh at them.

The most desirable personality trait in Japanese children is obedience. A famous Japanese proverb states: "The nail that sticks up will be hammered down." This means that anyone too unusual in behavior will be rejected by his or her friends and family. The person will be accepted when he or she changes to meet the group's expectations.

Changes in the Family

Until the past few decades, marriage was usually arranged between two Japanese families. Today, about half of all Japanese marriages are still arranged. But sons and daughters who choose their own marriage partners still often ask for their parents' approval.

Usually, boys and girls don't date until late in high school or after. They are too busy preparing for difficult college entrance exams to take time for dates. After college, men are busy starting their careers, so they often don't take time to date either. They find it is easier to let their parents find wives for them.

Unlike in the past, Japanese people today are marrying at much older ages. The average age at which men marry is about thirty years old, and the average age for women is twenty-six.

Another characteristic of the changing family is its size. Before World War II, a Japanese nuclear family—a father, a mother, and their children—was large. But today, Japan has the lowest birthrate in the world, and one-child families are common.

The birthrate has declined in both the rural areas and in the cities. Modern machines do most of the work on farms, so farmers don't need a large number of children anymore to help with all of the work. In the cities, it is impractical to have large families. Housing is hard to find, space is limited, and children are expensive to raise and to educate well.

Parents' Roles

Today, more than half of all married Japanese women work because living costs are so high in the cities. To make sure that children are taken care of while their mothers work, Japan has built an elaborate day-care system. In 1985, for example, there were almost twenty-three thousand day-care centers operated by the government, with about 1.8 million children attending. Besides these, there were more than fifteen thousand preschools operated by the Ministry of Education, with as many as 2 million children enrolled.

To help out with child care, private child-care services are becoming popular. One of these is the Japan Baby-Sitter Service in Tokyo. It has more than four hundred nannies who go to people's houses to baby-sit while the parents are at work. The Poppins Nanny School offers a three-month training program for people who want to be professional baby-sitters. The school teaches courses in medicine, nursing, child psychology, speech, manners, *origami*, and other skills.

Japanese mothers who work go home immediately after their workday ends, to tend to their children. Their primary afternoon responsibility is supervising their children's homework. Japanese mothers assume complete responsibility for their children's success in school. They consult teachers, choose schools, supervise homework, and check on their children's grades constantly. Japanese mothers are known as *kyoiku mamas,* or "education mamas."

Most fathers work much longer hours than their

wives. After work, they frequently go to clubs with other employees from their office and have drinks. In order to be popular with their bosses, many men drink with their fellow workers almost every night. As a result, many Japanese men have drinking problems.

Many of these men work on Saturdays as well. For this reason, some children see very little of their fathers. But because they want to see more of their families, Japanese fathers today are beginning to change. They are trying to work fewer hours and take more vacations with their wives and children.

Cooking Japanese

The Japanese diet has changed dramatically since World War II. The recent changes in the people's diet—such as eating eggs, beef, and chicken—have come from American influences. Dairy products and bread are also new additions to Japanese daily menus.

The people are growing taller from these changes in their eating habits. The average Japanese child today is four inches taller than the average Japanese child in the 1940s. The average seventeen-year-old Japanese boy today is 5 feet, 8 inches (174 centimeters) tall and the average seventeen-year-old girl is 5 feet, 3 inches (162 centimeters) tall.

Fast-food restaurants have introduced another change

People stroll through a food market.

to the people's diet. The Japanese are busy people and millions regularly eat fast-food on the run. American fast-food restaurant chains—such as Kentucky Fried Chicken, Wendy's, and McDonald's—are everywhere in the metropolitan areas.

In spite of all these menu changes in recent decades, traditional Japanese foods remain favorites in the country. Fish and rice are still the most popular foods eaten today. *Sushi* and *soba* are so popular that restaurants specializing in these two foods are found everywhere in the cities. Sushi usually consists of raw fish, rice with vinegar, and

A traditional Japanese meal.

a horseradish sauce. It can be served with vegetables,
flavored seaweed, or eggs. Sushi chefs take great pride
in their work, including decorating the sushi bowls with
cut bamboo and leaves.

   Soba noodles are long, thin, brown-colored noodles
made from buckwheat, so they are very healthful. Soba
is eaten year-round (often as a substitute for rice) but
always at New Year's, too, because it represents a long
life. The water from boiled soba is also used to make
soup.

   Another traditional Japanese food—commonly eaten

for breakfast—is *misoshiru,* a soup made of fermented soybean paste and hot water. Rice and pickled vegetables are also common breakfast foods. But some Japanese people today also eat eggs and toast in the morning, following the American tradition.

Here is a traditional Japanese meal that you can make yourself—a soup, *tempura* with rice, and a dessert. Tempura (fish and vegetables fried in batter) is a dish frequently eaten in Japanese homes.

Misoshiru Soup

1 cake *tofu* (bean curd)
2 tablespoons *dashi* (Japanese soup stock) or chicken broth
3 cups water
2 tablespoons *miso* paste
6 fresh okra (eggplant, potato, or another vegetable may be substituted for the okra)

☛Cut the tofu into half-inch cubes and drain the cake. In a saucepan, add the dashi to the water. ☛Put the saucepan on a burner and turn on the heat to medium. ☛Add the miso paste and stir well until dissolved. ☛Heat the soup for 2 to 3 minutes, but do not boil. ☛Add the drained tofu. ☛Rub the okra with salt. ☛Place the okra in a separate pan of rapidly boiling water. Let boil until the okra turns bright green and partly tender. Drain the okra and cut into quarter-inch slices. Discard the tips. ☞Add the okra to the miso stock and boil until cooked well. ☞Serve the soup hot. Serves 4.

Tempura

Several kinds of vegetables (green peppers, green beans, carrots, mushrooms, onion slices, summer squash or zucchini, sweet potatoes, eggplant)
1/2 cup dashi or chicken broth
3 tablespoons soy sauce
1/4 cup cooking sherry or *sake*
1 lemon
1 cup ice water
1 egg
1 cup flour
cooking oil
grated white radishes and scallions
cooked rice

☞Prepare the vegetables for frying. (Use enough so that each person can try several kinds.) ☞Cut the green peppers and carrots into long slices. ☞Cut the mushrooms in half. Cut the eggplant into half-inch slices, then cut each slice into four parts. ☞In a saucepan, make the sauce, combining the dashi, soy sauce, cooking sherry or sake, and a generous squeeze of lemon juice.

☞In a mixing bowl, make the batter by adding water and a lightly beaten egg to the flour. Mix well. ☞Add more water if the flour remains powdery. The mixture should look like thick pancake batter.

☞Fill a small frying pan with about 1 inch of vegetable oil. Warm the oil over low heat. ☞Test the heat of the oil by dropping a small bit of batter into it. The batter should fall to the bottom, be immediately surrounded by bubbles, then rise quickly to the top. If this does not happen quickly, the oil is not hot enough for cooking. Be careful not to let the oil burn, or the tempura will have a bad flavor.

☞Dip the vegetables in the batter, covering them completely. Then drop them into the oil. Turn the vegetables once, but don't wait until their coating of batter turns brown, or they will be overcooked. Take the vegetables out of the pan when they are crisp.

☞Place them on paper towels to soak up excess oil. Cover the tempura with the sauce, to taste. ☞Sprinkle grated radishes and scallions on top of the sauce to taste. Serve the tempura with side dishes of cooked rice.

Twice-Cooked Egg Cake

This sweet dessert is often made in Japan at New Year's for a holiday treat, but it is also eaten year-round.

5 eggs
7 tablespoons sugar
salt
1 teaspoon powdered tea

☛Hard-boil the eggs for 10 minutes, or until eggs are completely hard-boiled. Cool the eggs, then peel them. Separate the whites from the yolks. ☛Using the back of a wooden spoon, mash the whites. Then mash the yolks in a separate dish or bowl. ☛To the yolks, add 5 tablespoons sugar and a pinch of salt. Mix well. ☛To the whites, add 2 tablespoons sugar and a pinch of salt. Mix well. ☛Combine the powdered tea with the egg whites. ☛In a 5 x 9-inch (13 x 23-centimeter) loaf pan, spread the egg white mixture in an even layer. ☛On top of this, spread the egg yolk mixture in an even layer. ☛Cover the pan with foil and pierce the foil with a fork in several places. Place the loaf pan in a larger baking pan that is partly filled with hot water. ☛Bake in a preheated oven at 400° F (222° C) for 15 minutes. Cool the cake, then cut into 1 1/2-inch (4-centimeter) squares. Serves 4 to 6.

To serve this Japanese meal in traditional style, eat at a low table, use lacquer or porcelain dishes, use chopsticks, and drink hot tea. Enjoy!

7. Education for Success

While in elementary and secondary school, Japanese children are pressured by their parents and friends to get high grades. Not only do good grades help prepare them for college entry tests, but success in school also brings honor to their families.

In Japanese schools, great emphasis is placed on memorizing. Just learning to read and write Japanese takes many years of hard work. Although their spoken language is not like Chinese, the Japanese use Chinese characters called *kanji* for writing. By the time students finish elementary school, they must know 881 characters. Junior high students are required to memorize 1,850 more characters. By the end of college, students know about 5,000 characters.

The Japanese also place high value on self-discipline. This means they try to control their behavior so they can learn and improve their lives. In schools, students are taught that hard work, dedication, and sacrifice will lead them to success in life.

This discipline extends even to the students' everyday living habits, such as keeping their schools tidy. They dust and sweep their own classrooms. They also serve school lunches and clean up afterward.

Self-discipline is taught regularly in the schools' "moral education" courses. These courses teach the importance of politeness and justice. Students also learn respect for nature and public property, the individual's proper place in the group, and the advantages of working long hours. Students discipline themselves after school hours, too. Each evening, they spend at least two to four hours doing homework.

Discipline extends even to the students' physical appearance. In junior and senior high, they must wear uniforms. Boys wear black trousers and jackets with school badges on the collars. Girls wear dresses—dark blue in the winter and white in the summer—with pleated skirts and sailor collars. Unlike the boys, they do not have to wear caps.

The School System

The school year begins the second week of April and ends the following March. When the first term ends in late July, students enjoy their longest vacation. They don't start school again until the fall, in the beginning of September.

Their next break comes just after Christmas. This vacation lasts through the Japanese New Year's celebrations. Students return from this break the second week of January. The final term lasts until late March.

Then they have a couple of weeks off before starting their new school year.

Students attend school 240 days a year—Mondays through Saturdays—although Saturdays are only half days. But classes are not held on all of the 240 days. About 30 days are usually left open for field trips, sports days, and cultural events. The more important Buddhist temples and Shinto shrines are popular for field trips, as are well-known historical locations. Students also visit national parks.

After World War II, Japan adopted the same system as the United States—six years of elementary school, three of junior high, and three of high school. School attendance is required of all Japanese children under age sixteen. Unlike in the United States, students must take placement exams to determine which high school they will attend. The better schools require high exam scores. Once in a high school, however, everyone normally passes, no matter what grades he or she gets in classes. This prevents those with less ability from embarrassment and bringing shame on their families. About 95 percent of the students in Japan who enter high school graduate.

Compared to the schools in the United States, Japanese classes are large, averaging about forty-two students. The school day is similar to that of schools in the United States. In general, the students attend forty-five-minute classes, beginning at 8:30 A.M. After lunch, they have two more lessons and the school day ends at 3:00 P.M.

Education of many Japanese children begins before elementary school. More than half of the country's four-year-olds attend preschool. At age six, all Japanese children enter elementary school, where they take courses similar to those taken by American students—language arts, arithmetic, science, and home economics. All students study art and music in Japan. By the time students get to junior high, almost all are able to play a musical instrument.

In junior high, students choose a few of their courses, but not many. Most of their classes are required courses that are similar to elementary school subjects. But now, the students also learn English. By the time they graduate from high school, Japanese students have taken at least six years of a foreign language, usually English.

After graduating from ninth grade, some students decide to attend technical colleges for five years to study engineering or merchant marine studies. Others attend vocational schools, although regular high schools also offer basic vocational courses such as business, agriculture, technical and industrial skills, home economics, fishery, and health. In 1985, about one-third of all high school students enrolled in vocational courses.

In high school, students take as many as nine courses each term. A typical course load might be Japanese,

High school students are usually hard at work during the school day.

social studies, mathematics, science, music, fine arts, physical education, homemaking, and English. By the time they graduate, all students have completed three years of math, including calculus. They must also study physics and chemistry.

Juku, or "Cram School"

Outside regular school hours, many high school students also attend *Juku*, or "cram schools." Cram schools help students prepare for college entrance exams. There are about thirty-six thousand Juku in Japan. The most popular times for attending Juku are Sundays, weekday afternoons, and weekday evenings. About one in five elementary school students and almost half of junior high school students also attend Juku. They prepare for entrance exams at respected junior high or high schools.

Parents sacrifice a great deal to send their children to these schools. The average monthly cost of sending one elementary school student to juku is about fifty-five dollars. For a junior high student, the monthly cost is about seventy-five dollars. The main course of study for elementary level students is math. Junior high students mainly study English.

After-School Activities

Studying takes up many hours each day, but most students also are involved in activities after school. They join cultural or sports clubs, such as photography, basketball, painting, drama, science, or music clubs.

Besides joining clubs, many students play instruments in their school bands and are active in sports. Baseball and soccer are very popular with the boys, but they also participate in martial arts, such as karate, judo, and kendo, as well as tennis and other sports. Girls play a variety of individual and team sports. They especially like volleyball and tennis, but they also participate in

Most students participate in extracurricular activities, such as sports or cultural clubs.

sports such as swimming, track and field, and basketball.

Preparing for University

The Japanese believe that graduating from a university is necessary to achieve success in life. To get into a national university, high school seniors take a series of difficult exams. This is known in Japan as "examination hell." About 15 percent of the students will take the exams over again because they prefer to get higher scores. Some students who are no longer in high school also retake the exams. With higher scores, they hope to be accepted by a better university or one that has well-known programs in certain fields. Tokyo University is considered the best school for most subjects, and is famous for training leaders in business and government. The competition to attend Tokyo University is so strong that most entering freshman students have taken the exams more than once.

Attending a university and paying for tuition, fees, and living expenses is costly. Families sacrifice a great deal to pay these fees since government aid to students is not very widespread. Students from poor and middle-class families usually have to work during the holidays to help pay their college expenses. Because most Japanese belong to the middle class and save their money to pay for their children's college expenses, the financial burden is equal for most families. However, figures do show a much higher rate of children from wealthy families attending universities than those from poor families.

Once students enter a university, graduation is almost guaranteed. The four years of college are a time for students to make social and business contacts that will help them throughout their careers. Sometimes, students will have several job offers before they graduate.

Women and Careers

Graduating from college is not as important for Japanese

women because they rarely get hired for career positions in business and government. The most common jobs open to women are still in fields traditionally considered women's work—elementary school teaching and fashion designing. Today, many of the assembly workers in industries, such as electronics, are women.

Some women work at office jobs for a few years after college. But these jobs carry very little prestige. Often, these women do little more than pour tea or greet guests.

Most women who go to college attend junior colleges. These two-year schools specialize in vocational education. More than 75 percent of the students in these schools are women. The popular fields of study are home economics, teacher education, nursing, literature, business, and political science. Because the number of women graduating from four-year universities is still low, it is difficult for them to find jobs leading to leadership positions.

Japanese society is changing, however. In the past, women had almost no opportunities for lifetime careers in business and government. Even after World War II, when women began to enter the workplace in great numbers, the only work most of them could find were noncareer jobs. Although the Japanese constitution guarantees women an equal chance for good jobs, the government recently passed a law making it easier for women college graduates to find good jobs that would lead to high-level positions.

Changes in Japanese Education

A common criticism of the Japanese educational system is that it stresses memory at the expense of creativity. Because the writing system takes so long to learn, the Japanese must develop good memories. High school and university entrance exams mainly test the information students have memorized during their earlier school years.

The Japanese realize that they place too much importance on memorizing facts. Recently, the Japanese education ministry decided to encourage more creative thinking in classrooms. It has established new courses to be introduced in schools which will encourage problem solving and reward independent thinking.

To its credit, the Japanese educational system has produced a highly educated population. Japan has the highest literacy rate in the world—about 99 percent. The rate in the United States, by comparison, is between 80 percent and 90 percent. The excellent Japanese school system has provided its nation's businesses and industries with skilled workers who are responsible for Japan's economic success.

8. Sports, Games, and Vacations

Many sports in Japan began centuries ago as contests between samurai warriors testing their fighting ability. Wrestling, fencing, archery, and the martial arts were some of these sports, and they are still popular in Japan today. However, the Japanese are also active in sports introduced from other countries. They compete with other nations in track and field, basketball, soccer, volleyball, swimming, and many other sports.

Baseball Fans

Japan's most popular sport is *besuboru*, or "baseball." Baseball has been played in Japan since an American college professor introduced it in 1873. It grew so popular over the years that the country formed professional leagues. Today there are two leagues—the Pacific and the Central—with six teams in each league. Most teams are owned and sponsored by businesses. The Yomiuri Giants in Tokyo, for example, are named for the Yomiuri newspaper, and the Hankyu Braves in Nishinomiya (near Osaka) are named for the Hankyu railroad company.

Stadiums are usually filled with crowds of forty thousand or more for professional games. For the 1989 season, total attendance for both leagues was more than twenty million. In the stadium, fans dress up in team colors and wave banners. Bands play and cheerleaders lead thousands of fans in singing pep songs and yelling loudly for their favorite teams. Fans keep score on their scorecards, eat sushi and *hotto doggu* (hot dogs), and drink sake and beer.

Baseball is so popular that even high school games are followed closely. Each year, two high school baseball tournaments determine national championships. These games are covered by national television and newspapers, and fans fill the stadiums to support their teams.

An American all-star team toured Japan in 1934 with players such as Lou Gehrig, Jimmie Foxx, Lefty Gomez, and Babe Ruth. Since then, many well-known Americans have played for Japanese teams, including Don Zimmer and Davey Johnson.

Most star players, however, are Japanese. The two most popular in history were Sadaharu Oh, the son of a Taiwan immigrant, and Shigeo Nagashima. Oh hit 868 home runs while playing for the Yomiuri (Tokyo) Giants between 1959 and 1980. Nagashima played third base for the Giants and later managed them. He was not only a great hitter and fielder while playing, but he was a very successful manager.

As in all parts of their lives, the Japanese stress group loyalty in baseball. Team members pray together at a

Shinto shrine at the start of each season, and they are usually close friends with one another. In the off-season, they meet together for social occasions, too.

Players are very polite on the field. They bow to the umpire before stepping into the batter's box and apologize if they make an error or slide into another player. They are expected not to brag about their playing and not to embarrass one another in any way.

The players also apologize to their fans after losing a game. In 1975, the Yomiuri Giants finished last. The team officials sent out thousands of New Year's cards apologizing to fans for the team's poor performance.

Sumo Wrestling

Sumo wrestling, an ancient sport, is almost as popular as baseball. Matches were held centuries ago at local Shinto shrines during rice planting and harvest seasons as a way of pleasing the gods.

Today, there are six major tournaments every year. Each one lasts fifteen days, and each wrestler fights one bout per day. The matches usually last less than a minute. As soon as one of the wrestlers is pushed out of the ring or onto the floor, the match is over.

The wrestling ring is fifteen feet in diameter and elevated in the middle of the arena. The wrestlers wear only long cloths that wrap around their waists, hips, and

Sumo wrestlers.

thighs. When the two competing wrestlers enter the ring, they toss salt in the air to purify themselves and the ring. Then they raise their feet high and stamp several times to drive away the demons or evil spirits. Just before beginning the match, they clap their hands twice and show their palms to prove they carry no concealed weapons. After their brief bout, the wrestlers bow politely and walk back to their dressing rooms.

Wrestlers begin training in their teens. They move into a training "stable" that has dormitories, a cafeteria, and a gymnasium. In Tokyo alone, there are thirty-five stables with more than seven hundred wrestlers. The young men can enter after they complete junior high school. But they must begin as servants, preparing food and cleaning the gyms. Years later, by the time they are ready for professional competition, these same wrestlers usually weigh more than three hundred pounds.

Judo, Volleyball, and Golf

Many Japanese would claim that judo is Japan's best-known sport. It is taught to boys and girls in schools and practiced by millions of Japanese throughout life. *Ju* means "gentleness," and *judo* means "the way of gentleness." The goal is to defend oneself without resisting the opponent. When attacked, defenders do not use weapons or fight back with force. Instead, they turn aside and allow the attackers to fall off balance. The defenders can then easily throw or trap their opponents. Judo tournaments for all ages are held everywhere in Japan. The sport has become so popular throughout the world that it has been an Olympic event since 1964.

Volleyball is another favorite sport in Japan. It became even more popular after Japan won the 1964 Women's Olympic gold medal in volleyball. In Japan, women's leagues play year-round, and matches are usually broadcast on television across the country.

Golf, too, is becoming a major sport in Japan. There are driving ranges everywhere in major cities, even along riverbanks. Many of these driving ranges are crowded with men and women by 6:30 on weekday mornings. Fees to play on courses are usually extremely high, as much as fifty dollars or more to play fifteen holes.

Climbing Mount Fuji

Until this century, many Japanese considered it a religious duty to climb Mount Fuji at least once. Today, it is still a popular recreational activity and the mountain is crowded with climbers during the summer months.

Many climbers stay at hotels on the mountain, a few thousand feet from the top. They wake up early in the mornings, hike to the thousand-foot-deep crater at the top of the mountain, and watch the sun rise. This is called

These tourists "glide and slide" through the volcanic cinders on Mount Fuji.

Goraiko—"watching the sunrise from the mountain."

On clear mornings, the people at the top of Mount Fuji can see the outlines of Tokyo's skyscrapers and the lakes near the city. Looking north, west, and south, they see rice fields and rolling mountains.

When returning to Mount Fuji's base, many people choose to take the "lava slide." Because Mount Fuji is a volcano, some of its surface is made up of loose volcanic cinders about ten inches (twenty-five centimeters) deep. Using long, thick poles to keep their balance, people return down the mountain by stepping through the lava slide. The experience is similar to skiing down an easy slope and is often called "Glide and Slide."

Fun and Games

Japanese children today still enjoy many of the same games that their parents and grandparents did years ago, such as kite flying. Japanese girls today also take small, square pieces of paper and fold them into tiny animals, dolls, boats, and other objects. This ancient paper-folding pastime is called origami. A favorite origami animal to make is the crane, a symbol of long life.

Boys and girls also play age-old card games. One is called *irohagaruta* and dates back to the sixteenth century. There are two sets of forty-eight cards. One set has a proverb—a brief, wise saying—on each card. The second set has pictures illustrating proverb themes. The picture cards must be matched with the correct proverb cards. The player who matches the most wins the game.

Another traditional game that remains popular today is the board game *Go*. Go is played on a board with nineteen vertical and nineteen horizontal lines. These lines cross each other and form 361 intersections. Two players—one with 181 black stones and the other with 180 white stones—try to capture territory by surrounding space on the board with their stones. Each player usually has several "battles" going on at the same time.

Kite flying has been a popular Japanese game for generations. This kite painter designs and sells many beautiful kites.

Besides traditional card and board games, modern-day electronic games are popular with Japanese children. The game Nintendo was invented by the Japanese. The main character of the "Super Mario Bros." game was so popular that he was on stationery and other children's products. About one out of every four households owns a computer made by Nintendo Company—computers made just for playing games.

Vacation Days

In Japan, August is vacation month. Instead of traffic jamming the streets and thousands of people crowding the sidewalks in major cities, these urban areas seem almost empty. Only popular tourist cities such as Kyoto are busier in August.

The Japanese love to get away from work and school at the end of the summer. Millions go to the beach. Younger Japanese like to show off their latest swimsuits and clothes. The people also enjoy touring historical places.

The Japanese enjoy visiting modern amusement parks, too. Disneyland opened in Tokyo in 1983, and it has drawn more than 10 million visitors each year since. The record crowd for one day was 146,000 visitors who attended the 1987 New Year's Eve party.

Although they like the rides and exhibits at Disneyland, the Japanese people especially enjoy having their pictures taken with Mickey Mouse, Donald Duck, and other Disney characters. On their way home or back to their vacation hotel rooms, many Japanese stop at fast-food restaurants to eat. About three dollars buys a cheeseburger, french fries, and a Coke at one of the 704 McDonald's in Japan. Other people returning from Disneyland are just as likely to stop at a typical Japanese restaurant, where they leave their shoes at the door and sit on floor cushions to eat a traditional meal.

Living a life of such great variety—McDonald's and sushi, baseball and sumo wrestling—would likely be difficult for many Americans. But for the Japanese, it is natural. The Japanese have been able to mix old customs and new ideas with great success in all areas of their lives, including their sports, games, and vacations.

9. *Japanese in the United States*

The first Japanese immigrants who came to the United States worked on Hawaiian sugar plantations. They arrived in the 1850s. Soon, other Japanese immigrants came to the mainland, the largest numbers settling on the West Coast. Most of them worked at low-paying jobs, with the railroads, in lumber camps, in the salmon fisheries, and on strawberry and tomato farms.

The 1890 Census reported about 2,000 persons of Japanese ancestry living in the United States. By 1900, the number had reached more than 24,000. By World War II, the number had grown to almost 127,000. All of these Japanese people came to America in search of jobs and a better life.

Although very few Japanese Americans became wealthy during this early period, most were able to provide for their families. They made a decent income because they worked long hours for their bosses or in their own businesses. Employers liked their Japanese employees because they were hardworking, intelligent, and honest. Japanese Americans had no trouble finding and keeping jobs because of this work ethic.

Some people on the West Coast began to complain that the Japanese were getting all of the jobs. The anti-

Japanese movement grew. In 1905, labor groups met in San Francisco to form the Asiatic Exclusion League to stop Japanese immigration. The Asiatic Exclusion League also asked Americans not to buy goods from Japanese-American businesses. In 1906, San Francisco required that all Japanese children attend special schools to separate them from other children.

Between 1913 and 1924, more restrictions were placed on Japanese Americans. California made it illegal for the *issei*—first-generation Japanese immigrants—to own, invest in, or rent land. In 1924, Congress passed a law forbidding any new Japanese people to enter the country. But worse treatment of Japanese Americans was yet to come.

Japanese Americans and World War II

On December 7, 1941, the Japanese bombed Pearl Harbor, Hawaii. Although Japanese Americans were not personally responsible for the bombing, dozens of newspapers on the West Coast called for the removal of all Japanese Americans from their homes. They were suspected of everything from sympathy for the enemy to spying, though no evidence was ever found that a Japanese American committed an unpatriotic act.

On February 19, 1942, President Franklin D. Roosevelt signed Executive Order 9066. As a result of

In 1942, these Japanese Americans waited for the bus to take them to detention camp.

this order, 110,000 Japanese Americans were moved from their homes on the West Coast to detention camps. They could only take with them what they were able to carry. They had to sell nearly everything else that they owned, including their homes, farms, and furniture. Many sold their farms for small amounts of cash. Other farms were taken over by the government and sold at auctions.

The camps were rows of barracks, surrounded by barbed wire fences and towers with armed guards. An entire family was usually assigned to just one room. Men who had close ties to relatives in Japan were often separated from their families and sent to camps with even more severe restrictions.

Japanese Americans in Combat

Tens of thousands of Japanese-American men fought for the United States during World War II. Most who enlisted were from Hawaii (where Japanese Americans had not been forced to live in detention camps) but thousands also came from detention camps on the mainland. The all-volunteer 442d Regimental Combat Unit was made up of Japanese-American soldiers who were born in the United States. The unit fought bravely throughout Europe. It received more battle decorations than any regiment in United States history!

Former Hawaiian senator Spark Matsunaga fought

President Harry Truman (the smiling man wearing glasses) presented the 8th Presidential Distinguished Unit Citation to the 442d in July of 1946.

with the 442d. He returned home a captain with a Bronze Star and two Purple Hearts. After the war he went to Harvard Law School and entered politics. Daniel Inouye, the senior Democratic senator from Hawaii, also fought with the 442d. He lost his right hand in combat while fighting with the unit.

Senator Daniel Inouye.

Japanese Americans Since World War II

The outstanding record of the 442d combat unit helped change the minds of some Americans who thought that Japanese Americans were unpatriotic. But progress in eliminating anti-Japanese laws came slowly. At last, in 1952, Congress passed a law allowing Japanese people who had not been born in the United States to become American citizens.

After World War II, another law passed that gave Japanese Americans the right to file claims for damages and losses during the removal from their homes. But the legal process was long and complex. Many Japanese Americans who settled in court agreed to accept a small percentage of the value of their losses. Out of $400 million worth of claims, only about 10 percent were paid. Not many Japanese Americans received more than a few thousand dollars. But most of them accepted whatever was offered them, because they wanted to forget the past and move on with their lives.

In the 1970s, a new federal law was passed, admitting that the United States government was wrong in placing Japanese Americans in detention camps. The law granted $20,000 to each camp survivor or to his or her immediate surviving kin.

In the decades following the war, second- and third-generation Japanese Americans again found jobs, raised families, and continued their education. By the 1960s, the average Japanese American had the highest level of education of any racial or ethnic group in the country. Today, Japanese Americans still rank highest among all American ethnic and racial groups in high school graduation rates.

Before the war, Japanese Americans were excluded from most professions. Since then, thousands have become doctors, teachers, and lawyers. Today, Japanese Americans continue to excel in business, academics, politics, and the arts.

Well-Known Japanese Americans

Because many Hawaiians have Japanese ancestors, when Hawaii became the fiftieth state in 1959, many of the government officials were Japanese Americans. In that year, the chief justice of the Hawaiian Supreme Court, Wilfred Tsukiyama, became the highest elected Japanese-American official in the United States.

Patsy Takemoto Mink was a Hawaiian congresswoman between 1958 and 1977. Since then she has led a group—Americans for Democratic Action—that works for political reform. Besides Senators Inouye and Matsunaga, other well-known Japanese Americans from Hawaii are Governor George Ariyoshi and Congresswoman Patricia Saiki.

California also has many well-known Japanese Americans. Congressman Norman Mineta served as mayor of San José. Former senator and college professor Doctor S. I. Hayakawa was president of San Francisco State College for many years.

Japanese Americans have become famous in other fields as well. George Nakashima of Pennsylvania has become a nationally known furniture maker. Seiji Ozawa is known the world over as the musical director of the Boston Symphony Orchestra.

One thing is certain. Japanese Americans are an important minority group in the United States. They seem to do well in any field they choose to enter. Their inherited, centuries-old values—hard work, family pride, and respect for nature and their country—make them fine contributors to American Society. Japanese Americans are part of the United States' hope for a better future.

Appendix

Japanese Consulates and Embassies in the United States and Canada

Japanese embassies and consulates offer information and assistance to Americans and Canadians who want to learn about Japan or visit there. Contact the embassy or consulate nearest you for more information.

U.S. Embassy and Consulates

Chicago, Illinois
Consulate General of Japan
737 North Michigan Avenue
Suite 1100
Chicago, IL 60611
Phone (312) 280-0400

Houston, Texas
Consulate General of Japan
First Interstate Bank Plaza
1000 Louisiana Street, Suite 5420
Houston, TX 77002
Phone (713) 652-2977

Los Angeles, California
Consulate General of Japan
250 East First Street
Los Angeles, CA 90012
Phone (213) 624-8305

New York, New York
Consulate General of Japan
299 Park Avenue
New York, NY 10171
Phone (212) 371-8222

San Francisco, California
Consulate General of Japan
50 Fremont Street
23rd floor
San Francisco, CA 94105
Phone (415) 777-3533

Washington, D.C.
Embassy of Japan
2520 Massachusetts Avenue, N.W.
Washington, D.C. 20008
Phone (202) 234-2266

Canadian Embassy and Consulates

Ottawa, Ontario
Embassy of Japan
255 Sussex Drive
Ottawa, ON K1N 9E6
Phone (613) 236-8541

Toronto, Ontario
Consulate General of Japan
Toronto-Dominion Ctr., Suite 2702
P.O. Box 10
Toronto, ON M5K 1A1
Phone (416) 363-7038

Vancouver, British Columbia
Consulate General of Japan
1177 West Hastings Street
Suite 900
Vancouver, BC V6E 2K9
Phone (604) 684-5868

Glossary*

Amae (ah-mah-eh)—feeling of dependency toward another person.

Besuboru (beh-soo-bah-roo)—baseball.

Bonen-kai (boh-nehn-keye)—means "forgetting the year." Parties are held by businesses in Japan at the end of each year.

Bushido (boo-shee-doh)—code of the warrior. The samurai followed strict self-discipline and loyalty to their sponsors.

Chitose-amé (chee-toh-seh-ah-meh)—sweet "thousand-year candy" sold at shrines during Shichigosan.

Daimyo (deye-myoh)—wealthy Japanese landowners; they hired samurai to defend their lands.

Fukuwarai (foo-koo-wah-reye)—game in which a blind-folded player draws the features on an outline of a girl's face.

Futon (foo-tahn)—a cotton mattress about four inches (ten centimeters) thick, used for sleeping.

Go (goh)—board game of strategy. Players try to protect and capture territory.

Goraiko (goh-reye-koh)—"watching the sunrise from the mountain."

In Japanese, equal stress is usually placed on each syllable.

Hagoita (hah-goy-tah)—badminton.

Haiku (heye-koo)—three-line poem with 5-7-5 syllables, usually about nature and meaning in life.

Hanami (hah-nah-mee)—flower viewing; usually refers to cherry blossom viewing.

Hibachi (hee-bah-chee)—metal or ceramic pots used for heating homes.

Hinamatsuri (hee-nah-maht-soo-ree)—Doll's Festival celebrated by Japanese girls on March 3.

Hotto doggu (hoh-toh dog-oo)—hot dogs.

Hyakunin isshu (hyah-koo-neen ee-shoo)—traditional card game of matching poetry lines, played during the New Year's season.

Ikebana (ee-keh-bah-nah)—formal methods of flower arranging.

Irohagaruta (ee-roh-hah-gah-roo-tah)—card game matching proverbs and pictures.

Issei (ee-say)—first-generation Japanese Americans not born in the United States.

Ju (joo)—gentleness; *judo* means "the way of gentleness."

Juku (joo-koo)—private "cram schools" students go to after regular school to prepare for high school and college entrance exams.

Kabuki (kah-boo-kee)—dramatic art form in which actors wear colorful costumes and perform with lively movements, portraying everyday life.

Kadomatsu (kah-doh-mah-tsoo)—a decoration of pine branches set in bamboo baskets tied with rice-straw rope during the New Year's celebration.

Kanji (kahn-jee)—Chinese characters used by the Japanese.

Kimono (kee-moh-noh)—traditional wide-sleeved ankle-length Japanese clothing that wraps around the body.

Kodomo no hi (koh-doh-moh noh hee)—Children's Festival; see *Tango no Sekku.*

Koto (koh-toh)—string instrument played like a steel guitar but sounding more like a harp.

Kyoiku mamas (kyoy-ee-koo mah-mahz)—"Education Mamas," mothers who supervise their children's education closely.

Manga (mahn-gah)—comics.

Miso (mee-soh)—fermented soybean paste.

Misoshiru (mee-soh-shee-roo)—a soup made of fermented soybean paste (miso) and hot water.

Noh (noh)—dramatic art form in which actors wear masks and chant stories from Japanese history and mythology.

Origami (oh-ree-gah-mee)—art of taking small square pieces of paper and folding them into tiny, detailed objects.

Oseibo (oh-say-boh)—year-end gifts.

Sake (sah-keh)—rice wine.

Samurai (sah-moo-reye)—Japanese warriors.

Shakuhachi (shah-koo-hah-chee)—a seven-holed bamboo flute.

Shichigosan (shee-chee-goh-sahn)—"Seven-Five-Three Day" celebrated on November 15; parents pray for the health and happiness of their three- and seven-year-old daughters and five-year-old sons.

Shinkansen (sheen-can-sehn)—bullet train.

Shogatsu (shoh-ghat-soo)—New Year's festival.

Shogun (shoh-goon)—military rulers.

Soba (soh-bah)—a brown noodle made from buckwheat flour.

Sushi (soo-shee)—popular food usually made of vinegared rice, raw fish, and horseradish sauce.

Tango no Sekku (Tahn-goh noh sekh-koo)—Boy's Festival celebrated May 5; families display samurai dolls and equipment symbolizing the strength and fearlessness that children need to succeed in life.

Tempura (Tem-poo-rah)—popular dish made of fish or vegetables fried in batter.

Terebikko (teh-reh-beek-koh)—children who watch a great deal of television.

Tofu (toh-foo)—bean curd.

Torii (toh-ree)—used symbolically as an entrance to Shinto holy grounds; they are tall—often ten feet (three meters) or higher—and are usually painted red; consist of a crossbeam of wood (sometimes stone, concrete, or bronze) propped up by two vertical posts.

Waka (wah-kah)—term for Japanese poetry in general, and sometimes used for poetry called *tanka* (31 syllables of 5-7-5-7-7).

Selected Bibliography

Blumberg, Rhoda. *Commodore Perry in the Land of the Shogun.* New York: Lothrop, Lee & Shepard Books, 1985.

Dolan, Edward F., Jr., and Shan Finney. *The New Japan.* New York: Franklin Watts, 1983.

Ekiguchi, Kunio, and Ruth S. McCreery. *A Japanese Touch for the Seasons.* Tokyo: Kodansha International, 1987.

Japan in Your Pocket. 10 vols. Japan Travel Bureau, Inc., 1988.

Kim, Hying-chan, ed. *Dictionary of Asian-American History.* New York: Greenwood Press, 1986.

Meyer, Carolyn. *A Voice from Japan: An Outsider Looks In.* San Diego: Harcourt Gulliver Books, 1988.

Schwarz, Edward A., and Reiko Ezawa. *Everyday Japanese: A Basic Introduction to the Japanese Language & Culture.* Lincolnwood, Ill.: Passport Books, 1987.

Statler, Oliver, ed. *All-Japan: The Catalogue of Everything Japanese.* New York: William Morrow, 1984.

Index

About the Author

Tony Zurlo attended high school in Okinawa, Japan, and graduated from there in 1959. Since then, he has traveled extensively throughout Japan as both a resident and visitor. A university professor as well as a free-lance writer, Mr. Zurlo has taught college courses on Asian literature and on Japanese history and culture. The author has a number of newspaper and magazine articles to his credit, and he has published two books of poetry. *Japan: Superpower of the Pacific* is his first book for children. Mr. Zurlo lives with his wife in Arlington, Texas.